International Standard Bo(
(applies to this, th(

COLLEC(
GEORGE III
COINS

by

R. J. MARLES © 1997/1998

FARTHINGS	SHILLINGS	QUARTER GUINEAS
HALFPENNIES	EIGHTEEN PENCES	THIRD GUINEAS
PENNIES	HALF DOLLARS	HALF GUINEAS
TWOPENCES	HALF CROWNS	GUINEAS
THREEPENCES	THIRTY PENCES	TWO GUINEAS
FOURPENCES	THREE SHILLINGS	FIVE GUINEAS
FIVEPENCES	DOLLARS	HALF SOVEREIGNS
SIXPENCES	CROWNS	SOVEREIGNS
NINE PENCES	SIX SHILLINGS	TWO POUNDS
TEN PENCES	TYPICAL TOKENS	FIVE POUNDS

A compilation of historical facts; pictures of The Coinage;
a selection of unoffocial and offical tokens, but chiefly:
averaged selling-prices drawn from dealers' lists,
auctions and numismatic magazines.

ROTOGRAPHIC PUBLICATIONS · 37 St. Efrides Road
Torre · Torquay · TQ2 5SG · U.K.

1738 At Norfolk House, St. James's Square, London;
George William Frederick was born at 7.30am on 4th June.

1750 Created Prince of Wales

1760 Proclaimed King 25th October.
"Born and educated in this country, I glory in the name of Britain".

Fondly nicknamed "Farmer George" he is said to have planted pieces of beef in his garden at Kew to demonstrate how more beef would be available if more was grown! (Possibly during a bout of Porphyria: a disease with results similar to madness.) The King's first attack of Porphyria was early 1764 from which he, seemingly, fully recovered.

The American War of Independence was a bitter blow, although he contributed to it by his reprisals which followed 'embroidered' reports from the colony. A second attack of Porphyria brought him low in 1789. He became quite deranged for almost three months. Again, however, he made a full recovery.

Another aggravation was the French Revolution and the fact that 'interested parties' were bent on the King's assassination. On 15th May 1798, a man standing next to him *received* a musket-ball. George refused to cancel his visit, that same day, to the Drury Lane Theatre. As he entered the royal box a shot was fired, missing him due to the intervention of a theatre goer, and a bullet struck the roof of the box. George advised the Queen and Princesses to keep back *"They are firing squibs for diversion and perhaps there may be more".* The audience broke into prolonged cheering and thrice sang 'God Save The King'.

His Golden Jubilee was held on 25th October 1809 and all seemed well. The following year, however, his youngest daughter, Amelia died of consumption and this triggered another attack of 'apparent insanity' from which he never recovered. He became blind, deaf and 'mad': a particularly cruel end for a lover of music, of arts, of science and of books; although he didn't think much of Shakespeare's *"stuff".*

THE COINAGE

There was no official copper coinage bearing the portrait of George III until 1770. A small issue, however, was made in 1762 and 1763 using dies of George II coinage dated 1754. Official coinage from 1770 was progressively melted down and used for light-weight counterfeits.

A Mint report of 1787 stated "but 8% of coin had some tolerable resemblance to the King's coin". Little or no *useful* action being taken, tradespeople again issued their own small change in the form of tokens. These were often inscribed "For Trade", "For Use of Trade" or "For Change Not Fraud". Most were genuine promises to redeem for equivalent coins of the realm. One of the major manufacturers of the tokens was Matthew Boulton F.R.S. at his Soho, Birmingham Mint. His ambition was to produce coins not easily, or profitably, counterfeited.

Boulton proposed:

1) That each coin should contain its intrinsic value of metal.
2) That a retaining collar be used, during striking, to ensure a constant diameter.
3) That the lettering be incuse (struck in) so that the broader, unprinted part would take the wear of everyday use.
4) The presses be driven by steam now that steam power was a practical possibility thanks to one James Watt.

Steam presses would provide massive power enabling superior strikings and greater output.

A Privy Council (considering the state of the coin of the Realm) asked Boulton to submit patterns for a half-penny. Boulton, with an eye on a possible Government Contract, offered to produce half-pennies at half the cost previously experienced by the Royal Mint.

Jean Pierre Droz, a skilled die-sinker, was hired to apply his expertise to the new coinage. Whilst his die-work was excellent, other 'contrivances' of his were disappointing and he was, liberally, paid off. Boulton and his assistants perfected the process but, to meet the deadline, had to have the patterns struck, in Paris, on a Droz machine.

He gets the contract .... see page 15

GRADING TERMS

A "good" coin is so worn that most of the detail has disappeared. These are not featured: only very rare specimens have any value.

FINE — A coin worn by considerable use, but still retaining clear lettering and some of the finer detail (hair, for example, not just a 'parting').

V.F. — The highest parts of a VERY FINE coin will show signs of its having been circulated. It must, however, possess a pleasing appearance devoid of disfiguring marks.

E.F. — An EXTREMELY FINE coin is almost perfect; close examination revealing traces of wear to the highest parts.

Unc. — UNCIRCULATED - unworn, as struck by the mint.

PROOF — is not a measure of condition, but a description of the method of manufacture. Certain exceptions apart; the field ("unprinted" part) will possess a mirror-like polish; the inscription, legend, or other design, will have a "frosted" appearance; the whole having an effect of great beauty which the smallest scratch will impair.

Excepting rare coins, the value of which is determined by the fact that nothing better is available, to be "collectable" a coin should possess (at least) the requirements of FINE given above. The 'head' should not be worn to a silhouette. The grading should never be qualified by "for its age": a FINE coin of 1800 should be no more worn than a FINE one of 1900 despite the hundred years age difference. The presence of ALL THE ORIGINAL DETAIL but with the highest parts barely flattened (new but 'shop-soiled') would be considered EXTREMELY FINE. Even uncirculated specimens will vie for honours according to freedom from mint bag-marks, brilliance etc., until the rare title of F.D.C. (fleur de coin) is awarded.

CLEANING and POLISHING

A dealer's or auctioneer's list will sometimes indicate that a coin has been cleaned; a lower price results: the lesson should be clear. Cleaning diminishes value; polishing will TOTALLY DESTROY.

Date	Mintage	Peck No.	Fine	V.F.	E.F.	abt Unc/FDC

LONDON MINT

DATE BELOW BRITANNIA

COPPER: 23/24mm · edge plain

Date	Mintage	Peck No.	Fine	V.F.	E.F.	abt Unc/FDC
1771		P909	£20	£40	£120	£240/£360
1771	1st 7 struck over 1		(1993)	"BU full lustre"		£295
1771	Proof	P910	---	---	---	£400/£600
1773		P911	£5	£10	£30	£60/£95
1773	No stop Rev.	P912	£8	£16	£50	£100/£150
1773	Obverse 2	P913	£6	£12	£36	£75/£100
1773	Obverse 2	P914	No stop Rev.	£25	£75	(1993)
1773	No stop after Rex		£8	£25		on Peck 914
1774	Obverse 1	P915	£8	£15	£45	£90/£135
1774	Obverse 2	P916	£14	noted (1991)		
1775		P917	£9	£20	£60	£120/£180
1775	Inverted A for V	∀ in GEORGIVS		(1995)	£95	---/---
1790	Pattern in silver	P1034	---	---	---	£650
1790	Pattern in copper	P1035	---	---	---	£450

Obverse 1 has row of breastplate scales, broken by rose at centre
Obverse 2 has a full, unbroken, row of eight scales

1760 Married to Charlotte Sophia of Mecklenburg - Strelitz 8th September
Crowned KIng on 22nd September

SOHO MINT (Birmingham) DATE BELOW BUST

COPPER: 21/22mm · edge grained (milled) diagonally.

Date	Mintage	Peck No.	Fine	V.F.	E.F.	abt Unc/FDC
1797	Pattern	P1199	(noted 1994)		---	£295
1797	Pattern	P1201	(1993)	---	---	£225
1797	Pattern	P1202	(1993)	---	---	£225
1798	Pattern	P1203	(1995)	£95	---	£250
1798	Pattern	P1204	(1993)	---	---	£220
1798	Pattern	P1212	(1992)	---	---	£200
1798	Pattern	P1215	(1995)	---	---	£280
1799	Three berries	P1279	£3	£9	£25	£50/£75
1799	Four berries	P1280	---	---	£70	£200/£350
1799	Proofs and Patterns abound, averaging				£250	to £400 FDC
1799	Proof	P1390	bronzed		£150	(noted 1996)
1799	Proof but with groove as currency			"gdEF"	£45	(noted 1994)
1805	Pattern	P1319	bronzed	---	FDC	£275
1806	Portrait 1	P1396	£3	£6	£20	£40/£60
1806	Portrait 2	P1397	£4	£9	£30	£60/£90
1806	Incuse dot	P1398	---	£20	£60	£120/£180
1807	Portrait 1	P1399	£4	£9	£30	£60/£90

Portrait 1 Curls of side whiskers in *incuse* (struck in) lines.
The two lower leaves of wreath each have overlapping strand of hair.

Portrait 2 Curls in *raised* lines; no overlapping hair.

1762 First child · 12th August · George Augustus Frederick · Future George IV

1763 Second child · 16th August · Frederick · Duke of York and Albany

Date	Mintage	Fine	V.F.	E.F.	abt Unc/FDC

SOHO MINT

HIBERNIA and HARP Reverse · DATE BELOW HARP

Date	Mintage	Fine	V.F.	E.F.	abt Unc/FDC
1806	Incuse circle on harp butt	£5	£10	£30	£60/£90
	Raised circle on harp butt	£3	£6	£20	£40/£60
	Proof, bronzed	(noted 1995)		"abtFDC"	£120
1806	Proof, bronzed, large letters both sides				FDC £375
1806	Proof, gilt copper, edge engrailed		---	---	£225
	Re-strike (later date) in silver			---	£250
		(noted 1993)		"FDC Superb"	£1,000
	Re-strike in gold		---	---	---

Proofs with pellet stop after HIBERNIA are re-strikes

			Fair	Fine	V.F.	E.F.

'VOCE POPULI' COINAGE 21 to 22mm

"VOCE POPULI" · "Voice of the People" coins, being unofficial, are tokens rather than coins. It is argued, however, that no matter what is used, even a button, provided it is acceptable for purposes of trade, then it is as good as a coin. The fact that the Voce Populi 'tokens' were struck from the dies of Mr. Roach (or Roche), a button maker, does nothing to refute that argument!

			Fair	Fine	V.F.	E.F.
1760	(A)	Having large letters and "loop"	£50	£100	£350	£750
1760	(B)	No loop at truncation of neck		----	----	----

(A)

(B)

HALFPENNIES

TYPE 1

TYPE 2

TYPE 6

TYPE 7

1766 Fourth child · Sept 29th · Charlotte Augustus Matilda · Princess Royal
Christy's first sale took place on 5th December

'VOCE POPULI' (Voice of The People) COINAGE 25 to 29mm

1760 Copper HALFPENNIES 25mm to 29mm of different weights and having "portraits" which vary in crudity of execution. Identification could be as much by the position of stops, or absence thereof, and the 'attitude' of Hibernia; as by the accepted nine distinctions of the obverse portraits or the eleven 'differences' which can be set out. For pictures of all nine types your attention is directed to Messrs. Spink's "The Guide Book to the Coinage of Ireland" by Anthony Dowle and Patrick Finn.

		Fair	Fine	V.F.	E.F.
TYPE 1	Young head	£20	£50	£100	£200
TYPE 2	Older 'sophisticated' head	£10	£40	£80	£150
TYPE 3	A square head	£10	£40	£80	£150
TYPE 4	Square with chin uplifted	£10	£40	£80	£150
TYPE 5	'I' rests on truncation	£10	£45	£90	£175
TYPE 6	Still square, but aggressive with 'I' touching truncation	£10	£40	£125	£250
TYPE 7	"Mouselike"; large leaves	£10	£40	£80	£150
TYPE 8	Disillusioned; large gap between 'I' and truncation	£10	£40	£80	£150
	Variety VOOE	£10	£40	£80	£150
	Variety VOOE (Noted 1993)		"nVF"	£105	----
TYPE 9	Elongated head	£15	£50	£95	£200
(10)	'P before (to right of) head'	£15	£60	£120	----
	(10) at auction 1996	---	---	"gdEF"	£110
(11)	'P below head'	£7	£50	£125	£200

(10) 'P before (to right of) head'

(11) Variety 'P below head'

1767 Fifth child · 2nd November · Edward · Duke of Kent

1768 Sixth child · 8th November · Augusta Sophia

HALFPENNIES

LONDON MINT

COPPER 29/30 mm

FIRST ISSUE · DATE BELOW BRITANNIA

Date	Peck No.	Details	Fine	V.F.	E.F.	abt. Unc/FDC
1770	Armoured/Cuirassed Bust		£6	£20	£75	£150/£225
1770	P893A	No stop reverse	£10	£30	£120	- - - - / - - - -
1770	P894			Proofs in silver		£1200
1770	P895			Proofs in copper		£575
1771	P896		£6	£20	£75	£150/£225
1771	P897	No stop reverse	£10	£30	£120	- - - - / - - - -
1771	P898	Ball below spear head		£20	£75	£150/£225
1772	P899	Reverse A	£6	£20	£75	£150/£225
1772	P900	GEORIVS (error)	£15	£40	£140	- - - - / - - - -
1772	P901	Ball below spear head		£20	£50	£120/195
1772	P902	Reverse B	£6	£20	£75	£150/£225
1772	P903	No stop reverse	£10	£30	£95	£175/£250
1773	P904		£6	£20	£75	£150/£225
1773	P905	No stop after REX	£12	£30	£95	£175/£250
1773	P906	No stop reverse	£12	£30	£95	£175/£250
1774	P907		£6	£20	£75	£150/£225
1775	P908		£6	£20	£75	£150/£225
1775	P908	(noted 1993)		"Superb Mint State"		£175
1788	P966	Gilt proof	- - -	- - -	- - -	£195
1795	P1044	"Cartwheel" pattern	(noted 1989)	£99	"abtEF"	- - - -

Reverse 'A' = Top of head has incuse coil of hair
Scroll at base of shield has *curved raised* lines.

Reverse 'B' = No coil of hair. Scroll at base of shield has *straight incuse* lines.

1770 Boston Massacre (British troops kill five civilians) · 5th March

Seventh child · 22nd May · Elizabeth

Date	Peck No.	Details	Fine	V.F.	E.F.	abt. Unc/FDC

LONDON MINT

COPPER 29/30 mm

Reverse HIBERNIA and HARP · DATE BELOW HARP

Date	Peck No.	Details	Fine	V.F.	E.F.	abt. Unc/FDC
1766			£4	£20	£75	£150
1769			£4	£60	£150	---
1769		(noted 1995)	"Almost E.F."		£125	---
1769		Head almost reaches rim	£8	£40	£95	£200
1774		Proof, long hair, curls below ribbon			£150	£400
1775		(DF584)	£5	£25	£85	£160
1775		(DF584) (noted 1995)		"Virtually FDC"		£450
1775		Proof (Seaby 6614) (noted 1997)			----	£500
1776			£15	£55	£130	£275
1781			£5	£25	£85	£150
1782			£5	£25	£85	£165
1782		Proof	---	---	£175	£350

1771 Eighth child · 5th June · Ernest Augustus · Duke of Cumberland

Spain cedes Falklands (uninhabited) to Britain

Date	Peck No.	Details	Fine	V.F.	E.F.	abt. Unc/FDC

SOHO MINT (Birmingham)

COPPER 30/31mm

THIRD ISSUE · DATE BELOW BRITANNIA

Date	Peck No.	Details	Fine	V.F.	E.F.	abt. Unc/FDC
1797	P1154	Pattern (noted 1988)		£135		----/----
1799	P1156	Gilt pattern (noted 1993)				FDC £340
1799	P1233	Gilt pattern (noted 1997)			£40	----/----
1799	P1234	Bronzed pattern (noted 1993)				FDC £95
1799	P1235	Copper pattern (noted 1997)			---	£125/----
1799	P1247	Bronzed pattern (noted 1992)				£110/----
1799	P1248	5 incuse gunports	£4	£7	£30	£45/£75
1799	P1249	6 raised gunports	£5	£9	£45	£75/£115
1799	P1250	9 raised gunports	£5	£12	£60	£100/£150
1799	P1251	Plain hull	£5	£9	£45	£75/£115
1799	P1252	Raised line, no gunports		£12	£60	£100/£150

1773 Ninth child · 27th Jaunury · Augustus Frederick · Duke of Sussex

Boston Tea Party · 16th December · 340 Tea Chests thrown overboard

Date	Peck No.	Details	Fine	V.F.	E.F.	abt. Unc/FDC

SOHO MINT (Birmingham) COPPER 29mm

FOURTH ISSUE · DATE BELOW HEAD

Date	Peck No.	Details	Fine	V.F.	E.F.	abt. Unc/FDC
1805	P1308	Silver pattern by W. J. Taylor	---	---	---	----
1805	P1309	Pattern by Taylor (noted 1993) "Virtually As Struck"				£175
1806	P1376	Olive branch, no berries	£3	£6	£25	£40/£65
1806	P1377	3 berries, Soho underlined	£3	£6	£25	£45/£75
1806	P1379	Proof, plain edged (noted 1993)	---	"F.D.C."		£165
1807	P1378	3 berries, Soho underlined	£3	£6	£25	£45/£75

SOHO MINT halfpennies have an edge milled in a deep groove; this gives the appearance of two halfpennies joined together.

HIBERNIA and HARP Reverse · DATE BELOW HARP · Copper 29mm

Date	Details	Fine	V.F.	E.F.	abt. Unc/FDC
1805		£3	£12	£45	£120
1805	Proofs,	---	---	---	£150/£200
1805	Proofs, bronzed	---	---	---	£95/£125
1805	Proof, gilt copper	---	---	£95	£150/£200

Re-strikes exist in silver, also in gold.

1774 Tenth child · 24th February · Adolphus Frederick · Duke of Cambridge

1775 Start of American War of Independence · British lose at Lexington

PENNIES

Date	Silver/No.		Fine	V.F.	E.F.	abt.UNC.
Obverse LAUREATE BUST · Reverse DATE DIVIDED BY CROWN · Silver 12mm						
1763	G3/1		£6	£12	£24	£45
1763	G3/2	Proof	(noted 1996)		£500	----
1766	G3/3		£5	£10	£20	£35
1770	G3/4		£5	£10	£20	£35
1772	G3/5		£5	£10	£20	£35
1776	G3/6		£5	£10	£20	£35
1779	G3/7		£5	£10	£20	£35
1780	G3/8		£5	£10	£20	£35
1781	G3/9		£5	£10	£20	£35
1784	G3/10		£5	£10	£20	£35
1786	G3/11		£5	£10	£20	£35
1792	G3/12		£6	£12	£24	£50
1795	G3/13		£4	£8	£12	£24
1800	G3/14		£3	£6	£9	£18
1817	G3/15		£4	£8	£12	£24
1818	G3/16		£4	£8	£12	£24
1820	G3/17		£3	£6	£9	£18

1776 Eleventh child · 25th April · Mary

1777 Twelfth child · 3rd November · Sophia

...... continued from page 3

The hoped for contract, with the Government, was signed on 9th June 1797 with an order for 20 tons of twopences and 480 tons of pennies. The pennies to weigh 1 ounce (avoirdupois) and the twopences 2 ounces. Boulton had intended to make the 2d 1.5 inches in diameter so that 8 side-by-side would measure one foot; the 1d was to have been 1.412 so that 17 (!) would measure two feet. Eventually, and for no apparent logical reason, 2d x 5 = 8 inches and 1d x 5 = 7 inches.

Boulton fully expected orders for farthings and half-pennies and, accordingly, prepared patterns. No such order was forthcoming but a repeat of 500 tons of 1ds and 2ds was executed in 1798 but dated 1797.

Eventually, farthings and half-pennies were produced but the price of copper had risen such that the coins were to be of a reduced weight. The public was not informed of this and presumed it was being cheated. By the time the populace was ready to accept the 'underweight' coins, Boulton had abandoned the "Cartwheel" principle in favour of convex dies and edge graining (milling).

Chasing rising copper prices to maintain intrinsic value was found to be virtually impossible and official coinage itself became token coinage much as it is to-day.

The Soho mint being privately owned (not under the control of the Royal Mint) meant that Boulton could indulge himself, to show off his skill and the quality of his presses. This he did very readily, for collectors or for special gifts to friends. C. W. Peck mentions *Pièces de Plaisir* struck in copper, bronzed copper, copper gilded before striking, silver-plated copper, tin, pewter and, of course, gold and silver. Nothing whatsoever to do with official coinage !

1778 Thirteenth child · 23rd February · Octavius

French/Dutch/American alliance · Britain declares war on France

Date	Peck No./Details	Fine	V.F.	E.F.	abt. Unc/FDC

SOHO (*Birmingham*) MINT — COPPER 36mm

DATE STRUCK INTO BROAD RIM — *THE "CARTWHEEL" PENNY*

Date	Peck No./Details	Fine	V.F.	E.F.	abt. Unc/FDC
1797	P1075/Bronzed proof	(noted 1996)		---	£250
1797	P1077/10 leaves in wreath	£8	£25	£75	£125/£200
1797	11 leaves in wreath	£8	£30	£90	£180/£250
1797	Many proofs: gilt, silvered, in tin and in silver				
1797	Proof in gold	---	---	"guesstimate"	£20,000

DATE BELOW HEAD — COPPER 34mm

Deep groove to edge suggests two joined coins

Date	Peck No./Details	Fine	V.F.	E.F.	abt. Unc/FDC
1806	P1325/Gilt proof	---		(noted 1996)	£250/£400
1806	P1327/Copper proof ship has no flag			(noted 1996)	£300
1806	P1328/Copper proof ship has a flag			(noted 1996)	£300
1806	P1333/Bronzed proof		abt EF £50		(noted 1990)
1806	P1342/Currency 'A' ★	£5	£12	£50	£80/£125
1806	P1343/Currency 'B' ★	---	(Seaby 1990)	£65	----
1806	P1349/Copper re-strike proof (inferior to original striking)				£200
1807	P1344/Currency	£5	£12	£50	£80/£125
1808	One known (Spink 1985 Mint £15000)		(Coincraft 1996 £35000)		

Varieties, proofs, patterns; extensive.

★ 'A' has incuse hair curl to right of knot. 'B' has no incuse hair curl.

1779 Captain Cook stabbed to death · 14th February

1780 Fourteenth child · 22nd September · Alfred

Date	Details	Fine	V.F.	E.F.	abt.UNC.
HIBERNIA and HARP reverse · DATE BELOW HARP · COPPER 34mm					
1805	Currency	£7	£20	£50	£150
1805	Proofs,	---	---	£95	£150/£250
1805	Proofs, bronzed	---	---	----	----
1805	Proofs in gilt copper	---	---	£125	£240/£350
	In original (metal) case of issue				£500
1805	Proofs (re-strikes?) exist in silver, and in gold				
1805	Proofs Gilt ¼, ½, 1d set. Noted 1993				"FDC" £800

PATTERNS

Date	Details	Fine	V.F.	E.F.	abt.UNC.
1789	· The 'UNION PENNY' bronze		---	£300	£3500
	large letters obverse and small letters date side				
1806	MULE of English and Irish dies		£72	£225	£600
1813	Pattern PENNY by Thomas Wyon		---	£250	£800
1813	Another pattern PENNY by Wyon		---	£250	£750

TWOPENCES (Half Groat)

Date	Silver/No.		Fine	V.F.	E.F.	abt.UNC.
Obverse LAUREATE BUST · Reverse DATE DIVIDED BY CROWN · Silver 14mm						
1763	G3/21		£6	£16	£25	£50
1763	G3/22	Proof	(noted 1996)		£600	----
1765	G3/23		£100	£250	£500	£900
1766	G3/24		£5	£12	£22	£40
1772	G3/25		£5	£12	£22	£40
1772	G3/26	2nd 7 over 6	£5	£12	£22	£42
1776	G3/27		£5	£12	£22	£40
1780	G3/28		£5	£12	£22	£40
1784	G3/29		£5	£12	£22	£40
Obverse LAUREATE BUST · Reverse DATE BELOW '2' · Silver 14mm						
1786	G3/30		£5	£12	£22	£40
1786	G3/31	large obv. letters	£6	£14	£25	£45
1792	G3/32	"Wire Money"	£10	£25	£50	£90
1795	G3/33	normal '2'	£4	£8	£12	£24
1800	G3/34		£3	£6	£9	£18
Obverse "BULL" HEAD · DATE BELOW HEAD · Silver now 13mm						
1817	G3/35		£4	£8	£12	£24
1818	G3/36		£4	£8	£12	£24
1820	G3/37		£4	£8	£12	£24

1782 United States recognised as independent · Alfred (14th) dies 20th Aug.

Fifteenth and last child · sixth girl · 2nd November · Amelia

Date	Peck No.	Mintage	Fine	V.F.	E.F.	Unc/nrFDC

THE *"CARTWHEEL"* TWOPENCE

DATE BELOW BRITANNIA STRUCK INTO BROAD RIM · Copper 41mm

Date	Peck No.	Mintage	Fine	V.F.	E.F.	Unc/nrFDC
1797	P1077	722,160	£10	£30	£95/£150	£250/£400
	P1077	(noted 1997)	---	---	"gd E.F."	£325/----
	P1077	(noted 1997)	---	£25	"verdigris spots obverse"	
1797	P1065	Bronzed proofs	(noted 1996)			£350/£500
	P1065		(noted 1997)		"nr. F.D.C."	----/£750
1797	¼d, ½d, 1d, 2d set				£850	(Spink 1986)

These were the first coins (copper currency) to bear the initials D:G: (DEI GRATIA : "BY THE GRACE OF GOD"). Designed by Küchler, they were struck on steam powered presses installed by James Watt at the Soho, Birmingham, refineries of Matthew Boulton.

"8 of these shall weigh 1lb and measure one foot" (but see page 15)

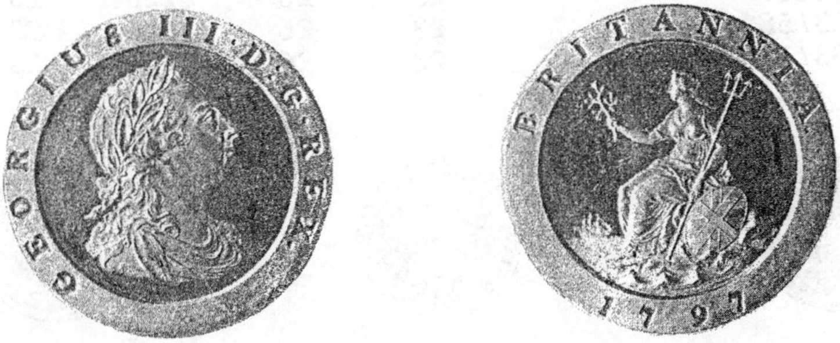

1783 Octavius (13th) dies 3rd May

Britain swaps Florida and Minorca for The Bahamas and Gibraltar

THREEPENCES

Date	Silver/No.		Fine	V.F.	E.F.	abt. Unc/FDC
Obverse LAUREATE BUST · Reverse DATE DIVIDED BY CROWN · Silver 18mm						
1762	G3/41		£4	£10	£20	£30/£40
1763	G3/42		£4	£10	£20	£30/£40
1763	G3/43	Proof	---	---	"guesstimate"	£1,000
1765	G3/44	extremely rare	£125	£300	£750	---/---
1765	G3/45	(noted 1991)	(Seaby, nearly E.F. £550)			---/---
1766	G3/46		£6	£16	£25	£45/£60
1770	G3/47		£6	£16	£25	£45/£60
1772	G3/48	large lettering	£6	£16	£25	£45/£60
1772	G3/49	plus very large III	£8	£20	£30	£50/£65
1772	G3/50	small lettering	£6	£16	£25	£45/£60
1780	G3/51		£6	£16	£25	£45/£60
1784	G3/52		£6	£16	£25	£45/£60
1786	G3/53		£6	£16	£25	£45/£60
Obverse LAUREATE BUST · Reverse DATE BELOW '3' · Silver 18mm						
1792	G3/54	"Wire Money"	£15	£30	£60	£75/£90
1795	G3/55	normal figure 3	£6	£16	£25	£45/£60
1800	G3/56		£5	£15	£20	£40/£55
Obverse "BULL" HEAD · DATE BELOW HEAD · Silver now 17mm						
1817	G3/57		£3	£6	£20	£30/£40
1818	G3/58		£3	£6	£20	£30/£40
1820	G3/59		£3	£6	£20	£30/£40

1784 Lt. Henry Shrapnel tests the invention named after him

1785 First balloon crossing of the English Channel

FOURPENCES or GROATS

Date	Silver No.		Fine	V.F.	E.F.	abt. Unc. / FDC
Obverse DRAPED BUST · Reverse CROWN DIVIDES DATE · SILVER 19.5mm						
1763	G3/61		£4	£8	£16	- - - / - - -
1763	G3/62	Extremely rare proof	- - -	- - -	- - -	£1.200
1765	G3/63	Rare currency	£125	£300	£750	- - - / - - -
1765	G3/64	E over R obverse	£200	£400	£900	- - - / - - -
1766	G3/65		£8	£16	£32	- - - / - - -
1770	G3/66		£8	£16	£32	- - - / - - -
1772	G3/67		£8	£16	£32	- - - / - - -
1772	G3/68	2 struck over 0	£10	£20	£40	- - - / - - -
1776	G3/69		£8	£16	£32	- - - / - - -
1780	G3/70		£8	£16	£32	- - - / - - -
1784	G3/71		£8	£16	£32	- - - / - - -
1786	G3/72		£8	£16	£32	- - - / - - -
Obverse OLDER BUST · Reverse DATE BELOW '4' · SILVER 19.5mm						
1792	G3/73	"Wire Money"	£12	£24	£50	- - - / - - -
1795	G3/74	Normal 4 from Maundy	£8	£16	£32	- - - / - - -
1800	G3/75	Also from Maundy	£6	£12	£18	- - - / - - -
Obverse "BULL" HEAD · DATE BELOW HEAD · Silver now 18mm						
1817	G3/76		£6	£12	£18	- - - / - - -
1818	G3/77		£6	£12	£18	- - - / - - -
1820	G3/78		£6	£12	£18	- - - / - - -

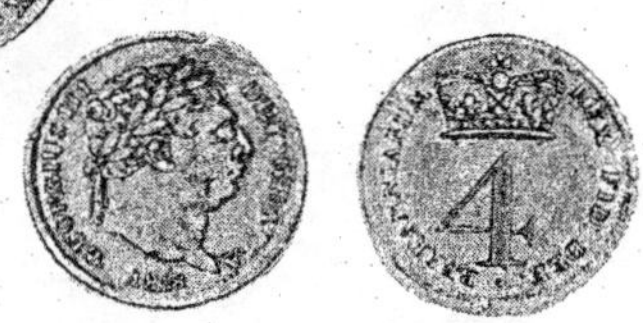

1786 Coal and Cotton create economic boom

1787 Foundation of The Association for the Abolition of the Slave Trade

Date	G3 No./Mintage/etc	Fine	V.F.	E.F.	abt. Unc/FDC
BANK of IRELAND OFFICIAL TOKENS · Obverse DRAPED BUST					
Reverse BANK TOKEN FIVE PENCE IRISH (Date below) · Silver 18.5mm					
1805	G3/BT1	£10	£20	£40	£75/£125
1805	At auction 1997	hammer price	"E.F."	£50	----/----
1806	G3/BT2	£6	£15	£50	£95/£150

1788 The King shows signs of insanity
The Commons debates a Regency but George recovers

Date	G3 No./Mintage/etc	Fine	V.F.	E.F.	abt. Unc/FDC
	Obverse DRAPED/ARMOURED BUST · Silver 21/22mm				
	Reverse DATE BELOW COMBINED SHIELDS and CROWNS				
1786	G3/81 Pattern - no hearts in Shield of Hanover				
1787	G3/82 No hearts	£5	£10	£15	£22/£30
1787	G3/83 Proof without hearts	--	---	---	---/£225
1787	G3/84 Proof, without hearts, on heavy flan			---	---/£500
1787	G3/85 With hearts	£5	£10	£16	£22/£30
1787	G3/86 Proof with hearts	--	---	---	---/£200
1788	G3/87 Pattern by Droz (ESC 1642)			£300	----
1790	G3/88 Pattern by Droz (ESC 1645)			£250	----
1790	G3/89 Pattern by Droz (ESC 1646)		(noted 1995)	£150	----
1791	G3/90 Pattern by Droz (ESC 1647)			£300	----
	Obverse "BULL HEAD" · DATE BELOW HEAD · Silver now 19mm				
1816	G3/91 Included below	£3	£9	£18	£35/£70
1816	G3/92 Proof (noted 1996)	---	---	---	£350
1816	G3/93 Proof in gold	---	---	"guesstimate"	£7,000
1817	G3/94 10,921,680 (inc 1816)	£8	£12	£25	£45/£80
1817	G3/95 Proof milled edge	---	---	---	£600
1817	G3/96 Proof, plain edge	(noted 1996)		£250	£400
1818	G3/97 4,284,720	£5	£10	£22	£35/£70
1818	G3/98 Proof	---	---	---	£750
1819	G3/99 4,712,400	£6	£12	£25	£50/£75
1819	G3/100 Proof	---	---	---	£450
1819	G3/101 Very small 8	£12	£20	£40	£60/£90
1819	G3/102 Proof 9 struck over 8		---	---	£450
1820	G3/103 1,448,960	£8	£15	£35	£60/£90
1820	G3/104 Proof	---	---	---	£350
1820	G3/105 Inverted 1 I820	£20	£45	£100	£150/£240

1789 Mutiny on the "Bounty" · 28th April

French Revolution gets under way on 14th July

NINEPENCES (Patterns)

Date	G3/No.		Fine	V.F.	E.F.	abt. Unc./FDC
Reverse BANK TOKEN 9D · DATE in WREATH of OAK and OLIVE · Silver 22mm						
1812	G3/BT3	(ESC 1478)		£150	£375	£600/£850
1812	G3/BT4	(ESC 1479) in copper		---	£400	£650/£900
1812	G3/BT5	(ESC 1480) silver '9 PENCE'			---	£700/£950

TENPENCES (Bank of Ireland)

Draped LAUREATE BUST · Reverse DATE BELOW inscription · Silver 22.5mm

Date	G3/No.		Fine	V.F.	E.F.	abt. Unc./FDC
1805	G3/BT6	First laurel leaf D E I ^ (below D)	£4	£20	£45	£95/£170
1805	G3/BT7	First laurel leaf D E I ^ (between D and E)	£4	£20	£45	£95/£170
1805	G3/BT8	First laurel leaf D E I ^ (below E)	£4	£20	£45	£95/£170
1806	G3/BT9	First laurel leaf D E I ^ (between D and E)	£7	£25	£65	£120/£180
1806	G3/BT10	First laurel leaf D E I ^ (below E)	£7	£25	£65	£120/£180

Obverse UNDRAPED LAUREATE HEAD similar to "BULL" HEAD · Silver 22.5mm
Reverse BANK TOKEN 10 PENCE IRISH · DATE in WREATH of OAK and OLIVE

Date	G3/No.		Fine	V.F.	E.F.	abt. Unc./FDC
1813	G3/BT11		£4	£12	£45	£70/£95
1813	G3/BT12	Proof of BT11	--	---	---	£150/£250
1813	G3/BT12	(noted 1993		"nrFDC"		£300
1813	G3/BT11	(noted 1994) Forgery: has '10' touching shamrock leaf				

1790 Launch of first purpose built lifeboat "The Original" · 30th January

1791 First edition of "The Observer" · 4th December

MAUNDY SETS

FACE VALUE TEN PENCE THE SET OF FOUR COINS · Silver

Date	G3/No.		Fine	V.F.	abt. E.F./Unc.
Reverse CROWN DIVIDES DATE					
1763	G3/81		£25	£50	£100/£150
1763	G3/82	A proof set of utmost rarity		---	---
1765	G3/83	Rarity equals that of 1763 proof			---
1766	G3/84		£25	£50	£100/£150
1772	G3/85		£25	£50	£100/£150
1772	(noted 1995)	(2d 7 over 6; 4d 2 over 0)		abt.EF	£100/----
1780	G3/87		£25	£50	£100/£150
1784	G3/88		£25	£50	£100/£150
1786	G3/89		£25	£50	£100/£150
1786	(noted Seaby 1988)		GVF	£60	---
Reverse DATE BELOW CROWNED VALUE					
1792	G3/90	★ "Wire Money"	£55	£100	£150/£250
1795	G3/91	Return to normal numbering	£20	£30	£60/£90
1800	G3/92		£20	£30	£60/£90

★ "Wire Money" because of the thin, 'wiry' script used for the figures 1, 2, 3, & 4.

Date	G3/No.		Fine	V.F.	abt. E.F./Unc.
Obverse DATE BELOW "BULL" HEAD · coins approximately 1mm smaller					
1817	G3/93		---	£40	£80/£120
1818	G3/94		---	£40	£80/£120
1820	G3/95		---	£40	£80/£120

1792 Introduction of Gas Lighting

1793 French Republic declares war on Britain · First "Fiver" issued 15th April

SHILLINGS

Date	G3/No.		Fine	V.F.	E.F.	abt Unc/FDC
DATED REVERSE AT TOP DIVIDED BY CROWN						Silver 26mm
1763	101	"Northumberland"	£150	£250	£400	£600/----
1763	101	(KB Coins 1994)	---	"gd EF"	£474	----
1764	102	Pattern (ESC 1238) (Spink 1988) "as struck"				£650
1775	103	Pattern (ESC 1239) very much rarer than G3/102				----
1778	104	Pattern (ESC 1240) (noted 1989)			£575	----
1786	105	Pattern, no stops at date or above head, much rarer than G3/103				

Upon his appointment as Lord Lieutenant of Ireland, the Earl of Northumberland distributed, in Dublin, some 2,000 pieces of this Young Head shilling.

Date	G3/No.		Fine	V.F.	E.F.	abt Unc/FDC
DATED REVERSE AT TOP DIVIDED BY CROWN						Silver 25mm
1787	106	No semée of hearts	£9	£15	£30	£45/£60
1787	107	1 struck over 'mirrored' 1	£50	£90	£140	£240/----
1787	108	Proof of G3/106, plain edge, thick flan			---	£600
1787	109	No semée, no stop above head		£20	£50	£70/£125
1787	110	Proof of G3/109	---	---	---	£350
1787	111	Plain edge proof of G3/109		---	---	£600
1787	112	Proof of G3/109 on heavy flan		---	---	£650
1787	113	No semée, no stops at date		£25	£60	£95/£150
1787	114	As G3/113 but 7 struck over 6		£25	£60	£95/£150
1787	115	No stops obverse	£70	£175	£500	----/----
1787	116	Proof, plain edge, of G3/115		---	---	£750
1787	117	Semée of hearts in shield	£9	£15	£30	£45/£60
1787	118	1 struck over 'mirrored' 1, with hearts			---	£750
1787	119	Plain edge proof of G3/117		---	---	£350
1787	120	Pattern (ESC 1241), with hearts, by Pingo			---	----/----
1787	121	Pattern (ESC 1242), royal cypher GR, by Droz				----/----
1787	122	(ESC 1242A) as previous but in brass				----/----
1798	123	★ Dorrien & Magens, no stop above head			(Seaby '97)	£3,500
1798	124	Pattern (ESC 1243) by Milton		---	---	----/----
1798	125	As G3/124 but in copper		---	---	----/----

★ Variously 'listed' as Mr. M. Dorrien Magens or Messrs, Dorrien, Magens, Mello, Martin & Harrison; a group of bankers/businessmen delivered a quantity of silver to the Mint and had coins, including shillings, struck from dies very similar to the existing coinage. One difference was the missing stop above the King's head. Lords of the Committee of Council prohibited their issue.

1794 The "Glorious First of June": French fleet defeated at Battle of Brest

1795 Holland sides with France so Britain takes Ceylon from the Dutch

Date	G3/No.	Mintage/etc.	Fine	V.F.	E.F.	abt Unc/FDC
NEW COINAGE · "BULL" HEAD · DATE BELOW HEAD						Silver 24mm
'1816'	131	Undated pattern by W. Wyon		---	---	----/----
1816	132		£6	£12	£25	£45/£65
1816	133	Proof	---	---	---	£700
1816	134	Proof, plain edge	---	---	---	£700
1816	135	Proof of G/132, in gold	---	---	"guesstimate"	£9,000
1817	136	23,031,360	£6	£14	£30	£50/£75
1817	137	Proof, plain edge, of G3/136		---	£400	£600
1817	138	GEOE (E over R)	£15	£45	£120	----/----
1817	138	(Colin Cooke 1995) "Mint state" "Finest known"				£475
1818	139	1,342,440	£15	£30	£85	£140/----
1818	140	Second 8 higher	£30	£60	£165	£300/----
1819	141	7,595,280	£6	£12	£30	£50/£75
1819	142	9 struck over 8	£10	£20	£50	£75/£125
1819	142	(Messrs. Weeks 1989)	---	"toned, gem unc"		£150
1820	143	7,975,440	£6	£12	£30	£50/£75
1820	144	Proof of G3/143	---	---	---	£350
1820	145	I of HONI struck over S	---	£20	£55	£80/£150
1820	146	H of HONI over ⌶	---	---	---	£500/----

1795 The future George IV married · 8th April

1796 French fleet scattered by storm whilst attempting invasion of Ireland

EIGHTEEN PENCES

Date	G3/No.			Fine	V.F.	E.F.	Unc/abt FDC
BANK OF ENGLAND TOKENS · DATED REVERSE · Silver 26mm							
Obv. ARMOURED BUST · Rev. BANK TOKEN 1s 6D IN OAK WREATH							
1811	G3/BT13			£9	£18	£36	£60/£80
1811	BT14	Proof	(noted 1996)	---	---	£225	£350
1812	BT15			£9	£18	£36	£60/£80
LAUREATE HEAD · Rev. BANK TOKEN 1s 6D · OAK/OLIVE WREATH							
1812	G3/BT16			£8	£16	£32	£50/£70
1812	BT17	Proof	(noted 1996)			£225	£350
1812	BT18	Proof with small lettering reverse			"guesstimate"		£1250
1812	BT19	Proof in platinum	(noted 1996)			---	£2,500
1813	BT20			£8	£16	£32	£50/£70
1813	BT21	Proof in platinum		---	---	---	£2,500
1814	BT22			£8	£16	£32	£50/£70
1815	BT23			£8	£16	£32	£50/£70
1816	BT24			£8	£16	£32	£50/£70

1797 14,000 French troops land in Dyfed but surrender to British soldiers

First copper penny minted and first £1 note issued

G3/No. Details Fine V.F. E.F.

HALF DOLLARS are, in the main, countermarked 4 reales of Spain. The latter are PIECES OF FOUR, which doesn't have the 'ring' of PIECES OF EIGHT. Other, half-crown sized, foreign coins were also countermarked and used to alleviate the chronic shortage of British coins. Dates are of original/host coins.

G3/No.	Details	Fine	V.F.	E.F.
Oval Countermark	ORIGIN		Silver 32 to 34mm	
G3/151	Spain	£95	£175	£350
G3/152	Spanish-America	£125	£250	£600
G3/153	Other than Spanish	£200	£450	£850
Octagonal Countermark				
G3/154	Spain	£125	£250	£600
G3/155	Spanish-America	£175	£350	£700
G3/156	Other than Spanish	£300	£500	£950

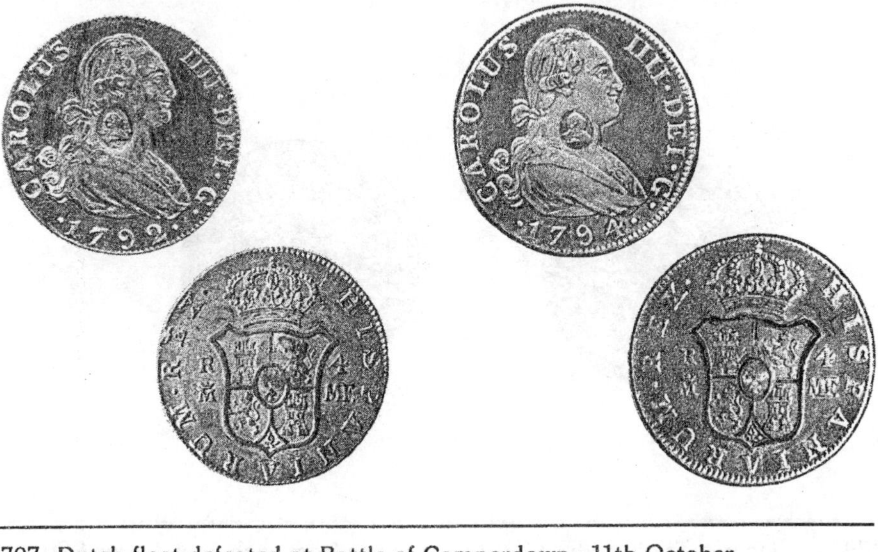

1797 Dutch fleet defeated at Battle of Camperdown · 11th October

1798 Nelson destroys 11 of 13 French battleships at Battle of the Nile · 1st Aug.

HALF CROWNS

Date	G3/No.	Mintage/etc.	Fine	V.F.	E.F.	abt Unc/FDC
Obverse "BULL" HEAD · DATE BELOW HEAD · Silver 32mm						
1816	161		£10	£30	£90	£180/£225
1816	162	Proof	---	---	---	£950
1816	163	Proof, plain edge	---	---	---	£1,000
1817	164	8,092,656	£9	£25	£75	£150/£200
1817	165	Proof	---	---	---	950
1817	166	Proof, plain edge	---	---	---	£1,200
1817	167	Proof in copper	---	---	---	£600
1817	168	D of DEI over T	£12	£45	£150	£225/£325

1799 Income Tax introduced at two shillings from each pound over £20

1800 James Hatfield attempts to assassinate GIII at theatre Drury Lane

HALF CROWNS

Date	G3/No.	Mintage/etc.	Fine	V.F.	E.F.	abt Unc/FDC
Obverse SMALLER HEAD · LARGER DATE BELOW HEAD · 32mm						
1817	171		£10	£30	£90	£180/£225
1817	172	S's (in motto) 'mirrored'	£15	£60	£175	£250/£350
1817	173	Proof	---	---	---	£950
1817	174	Proof, plain edge	---	---	---	£850
1817	175	Pattern (ESC 627) by T. Wyon		"guesstimate"		£1,500
1818	176	2,905,056	£10	£30	£90	£180/£250
1818	177	Proof	---	---	---	£1,400
1819	178	4,790,016	£10	£30	£90	£150/£200
1819	179	9 struck over 8	£40	£90	£350	£500/£700
1819	180	Proof	---	---	---	£950
1820	181	2,396,592 (inc GIV)	£15	£45	£125	£200/£300
1820	282	Proof	---	---	---	£950
1820	283	Proof, plain edge	---	---	---	£1,400

1800 British capture Malta

1801 Act of Union of Great Britain and Ireland creates United Kingdom

THIRTY PENCE

Date	G3/No.		Fine	V.F.	E.F.	abt. Unc/FDC.
HIBERNIA/HARP · BANK TOKEN · XXX PENCE IRISH · Silver 31/32mm						
1808	BT31	Harp 'points' to TOKEN ^ (under O)	£15	£40	£125	£200/£350
1808	BT31	(noted 1997)	"VF+"	£75	£125	£200/£350
1808	BT32	Harp to T O K E N ^ (under O)	£15	£45	£150	£300/ - - - -

1801 Nelson defeats Danish fleet at Battle of Copenhagen · 2nd April

1802 Candle-lit tunnel proposed to link Britain and France

THREE SHILLINGS

BANK OF ENGLAND TOKENS · ARMOURED BUST · Silver 34/35mm
Rev. BANK TOKEN 3 SHILL · DATE · OAKWREATH and ACORNS

Date	G3/No.	First leaf ^ points to ↓	Berries in HEAD WREATH ↓	Number of acorns in WREATH Reverse ↓	Fine	V.F.	E.F.	abt. Unc/FDC.
1811	BT33	D E^ I	· 5	· 27	£15	£30	£60	£120/----
1811	BT34	....			Proof	---	---	£500
1811	BT35	D E^ I	· 5	· 26	£10	£20	£40	£80/£120
1811	BT36	D ^ E I	· 5	· 27	Proof	---	---	£750
1811	BT37	D ^ E I	· 5	· 26	£30	£60	£90	£180/£250
1811	BT38	....			Proof	---	---	£600
1811	BT39	D E^ I	· 5	· 24	£30	£60	£90	£180/£250
1811	BT40	....			Proof	---	---	£600
1811	BT41	D E^ I	· 5	· 27	Proof	---	---	£750
1811	BT42	D E^ I	· 5	· 26	Proof	---	---	£750
1812	BT43	D E^ I	· 4	· 26	£12	£25	£45	£90/£125

Obverse LAUREATE "BULLISH" HEAD · Rev. WREATH OF OAK/OLIVE

Date	G3/No.	First leaf ^ points to ↓	Fine	V.F.	E.F.	abt. Unc/FDC.
1812	BT44	D E I ^ G R A	£12	£25	£45	£90/£125
1812	BT45	....	Proof	---	---	£500
1812	BT46	....	Proof in gold	"guesstimate"		£9,000
1812	BT47	D^ E I G R A	£90	£180	£360	----/----
1812	BT48	....	Proof in platinum		---	£6,500
1813	BT49	D E I ^ G R A	£12	£25	£45	£90/£125
1814	BT50	D E I ^ G R A	£12	£25	£45	£90/£125
1815	BT51	D E I ^ G R A	£12	£25	£45	£90/£125
1816	BT52	D E I ^ G R A	£12	£25	£45	£90/£125

DOLLARS

(4/9d; 5/-; or 5/6d !)

(Face Value 4/9d: thus "Two King's Heads not worth a Crown")

DOLLARS are, in the main, Spanish American 8 reales (pieces of eight), which have been countermarked for use as British currency. Other crown-sized foreign coins were similarly used. Dates are those of host coins.

Oval Countermark (from hallmark punch) — Silver 39/40mm

G3/No.	Details: ORIGIN	TYPE	Fine	V.F.	E.F.
G3/301	Bolivia *(Potosi)*	Pillar	£200	£400	£900
G3/302	....	Portrait	£100	£200	£425
G3/303	Chile *(Santiago)*	Portrait	£200	£400	----
G3/304	France	On an ECU	£450	----	----
G3/305	Guatemala	Portrait	£100	£200	£425
G3/306	Mexico	Pillar	£150	£300	£600
G3/307	....	Portrait	£80	£150	£300
G3/308	Peru *(Lima)*	Pillar	£180	£360	£750
G3/309	....	Portrait	£90	£180	£350
G3/310	Spain	Portrait	£200	£500	£900
G3/311	U.S.A.	(Bank of England collection)	Unique ?		Fine £2,500

"Pillar" Type:

Obverse Crowned Shield · Reverse 2 hemispheres between 'Pillars of Hercules"

1802 A certain Madame Tussaud brings her waxwork collection to Britain

1803 An army of 150,000 assembles at Dunkirk for the invasion of Britain

G3/No.	Details		Fine	V.F.	E.F.
Octagonal Countermark (from Maundy punch) · Portrait (bust of "Monarch")					
G3/312	Bolivia	....	£140	£300	£650
G3/313	France	(Bank of England collection)	Unique ?	----	----
G3/314	Guatemala	....	£450	£900	----
G3/315	Mexico	....	£90	£200	£450
G3/316	Peru	....	£250	£500	£950
G3/317	Spain	....	£300	£600	£1,200
G3/318	U.S.A.	(Seaby lists 5 genuine, 3 forgeries !)		----/----	

1804 Spain declares war on Britain

The British use shrapnel for the first time · 30th April

G3/No.				Fine	V.F.	E.F.	Abt. Unc.

Reverse BRITANNIA WITH SHIELD in OVAL GARTER · K (below shield)
FIVE SHILLINGS DOLLAR (on garter)
BANK OF ENGLAND (around rim) · 1804 below · Silver 41mm
Obverse LAUREATE BUST · First leaf of laurel wreath points to D E I
^

Obverse on truncation ↓		K below shield Reverse ↓	Fine	V.F.	E.F.	Abt. Unc.
G3/401	C. H. K.	K raised	£50	£95	£225	----
G3/402		Proof	----	----	----	£500
G3/403		Proof in copper	----	----	----	£300
G3/404	C. H. K.	ꓘ inverted/incuse	£100	£200	£400	£600
G3/405	C H K	K raised	£80	£160	£300	£450
G3/406		Proof	----	----	----	£600

Obverse LAUREATE BUST · First leaf of laurel wreath points to D E I
^

			Fine	V.F.	E.F.	Abt. Unc.
G3/407	C H K	K raised	£80	£160	£300	£450
G3/408		Proof	----	----	----	£450
G3/409		Proof in silver gilt	----	----	----	£750
G3/410		Proof in copper	----	----	----	£300
G3/411	C H K	ꓘ inverted/raised	£80	£160	£300	£450
G3/412		Proof	----	----	----	£500
G3/413		Proof in copper	----	----	----	£300
G3/414	C H K	ꓘ inverted/incuse	£80	£160	£300	£450
G3/415		Proof in copper	----	----	----	£600

1805 British win at Trafalgar, 21st Oct. · French win at Austerlitz 2nd Dec.
Rear-Admiral Sir Francis Beaufort compounds his wind scale

G3/No.			Fine	V.F.	E.F.	Abt. Unc.

Reverse BRITANNIA WITH SHIELD in OVAL GARTER · K (below shield)
FIVE SHILLINGS DOLLAR (on garter)
BANK OF ENGLAND (around rim) · 1804 below · Silver 41mm
Obverse LAUREATE BUST · First leaf of laurel wreath points to D E‸I

Obverse on truncation ↓	K below shield Reverse ↓		Fine	V.F.	E.F.	Abt. Unc.
G3/416	C.H.K.	K raised	£50	£100	£200	£350
G3/417	C.H.K.	ꓘ inverted/raised	£80	£160	£300	£450
G3/418		Proof	----	----	----	£500
G3/419		Proof in silver gilt	----	----	----	£750
G3/420		Proof in copper	----	----	----	£350
G3/421	C.H.K.	ꓘ inverted/incuse	£85	£175	£350	£500
G3/422		Proof in copper	----	----	----	£500

NO STOP AFTER REX (previously REX·)

			Fine	V.F.	E.F.	Abt. Unc.
G3/423	C.H.K.	K raised	£50	£100	£200	£350
G3/424		Proof	----	----	----	£500
G3/425		Proof on very thick flan	(noted	1993)	"FDC"	£3,500
G3/426		Proof in copper	----	----	----	£350
G3/427		Proof in copper on thicker flan		----	----	£500
	C.H.K. recut	(ESC 167) Proof, copper, very thick flan				----

Those struck on pieces of eight and still showing original date are worth more.
70 numbers have been reserved for the many patterns yet to be 'unravelled'.

1807 London partially lit by gas

The Slave Trade is abolished throughout the British Empire

CROWNS (Five Shillings)

PATTERNS — SILVER 38/39mm

It seems incredible that from 1760 to 1818 (although he could only have guessed it, George had but months left) that there had been no 'proper' crowns. There was such a plethora of trials and patterns perhaps 'they' just couldn't make up their minds or agree on what they thought was a suitable design. Of those many patterns, only those which have come up for sale are featured.

Year	Number	Description	Reference	Price
1816	G3/501	Trial crown using half-crown dies (EPP151) struck in copper	(1946 10 guineas)	(1965 £105)
(1816)	G3/502	Undated pattern by Webb and Mills		"appears frequently"
(1816)	G3/503	As previous but struck in lead		(EPP gives 1820 as date)
1817	G3/504	"The THREE GRACES" Perhaps 50 pieces	pattern by W. Wyon	(1980 £3,500)
1817	G3/505	3/4 in gold	(ESC 224)	----/----
1817	G3/506	4/5 in copper (EPP 154)	(ESC 225)	----/----
1817	G3/507	8/9 in white metal (EPP 155)	(ESC 226)	----/----
1817	G3/508	4/5 in lead on very thick flan	(ESC 228)	----/----
1817	G3/509	2/3 lead, smaller lion/thistle	(ESC 227)	----/----
	A set (3)	(silver, tin, encapsulated tin)	Spinks 1984	£12,500
1817	G3/510	18 The INCORRUPTA in silver by W. Wyon The X of REX 'collides' with drapes		(1966 FDC £750
	G3/510	(noted 1993) ----	"FDC"	£6,000
1817	G3/511	7 As previous but in gold		(1962 FDC £1,750)
1817	G3/512	1/2 By Pistrucci from unflawed die		----/----
1817	G3/513	3/4 From flawed die (die detroyed)		----/----
1817	G3/514	Incuse lettering between grained borders DECVS ET TVTAMEN · ANNO REGNI QUINQUAGESIMO Я SEPTIMO Attention is drawn to the 'R' punched the wrong way around		
1817	G3/515	Raised lettering between two fine borders DECVS ET TVTAMEN · ANNO REGNI LVIII	(ESC 233)	----/----

EPP = "English Proofs and Patterns" (see page 46)

1808 Start of Peninsula War

Wellesley's men defeat the French · 21st August

1809 Battle of Talavera · Wellesley's men again win The Day
Wellesley rewarded with the title Duke of Wellington

CROWNS (Five Shillings)

CURRENCY

Obverse LAUREATE HEAD · DATE BELOW

Reverse ST. GEORGE and THE DRAGON · Silver 38.61mm

Edge RAISED LETTERING · DECVS ET TVTAMEN · ANNO REGNI (date)

Date		Mintage	Date	Fine	V.F.	E.F.	Unc/abt. FDC
1818	G3/601	155,232	LVIII	£20	£55	£200	£350/£500
1818	G3/602	Proof	LVIII	---	---	----	£1,000
1818	G3/603		Incuse edge lettering			----	£1,250
1818	G3/604	Error edge	DECVS ANNO REGNI ET TVTAMEN · LVIII	£500	£1500	£3750	----/----
1818	G3/605		LIX	£20	£60	£225	£350/£500
1819	G3/606	683,496	LIX	£20	£60	£225	£350/£500
1819	G3/607	No stops at edge		£25	£90	£375	£500/£750
1819	G3/608	9 over 8	LIX	£25	£90	£375	£500/£750
1819	G3/609		LX	£20	£55	£200	£350/£500
1819	G3/610	No stop after TVTAMEN			£55	£200	£350/£500
1819	G3/611	Proof of G3/609		---	---	----	£1,000
1819	G3/612	Proof, plain edge		---	---	----	£3,500
1820	G3/613	448,272	LX	£20	£55	£200	£350/£500
1820	G3/614	Proof		---	---	----	£1,000
1820	G3/615	20 over 19		£25	£90	£350	£500/£750
1820	G3/616	S over T (SoiT)		£25	£90	£350	£500/£750

1810 Amelia (last born and great favourite) dies · 2nd November

King George III loses his sanity

1811 George III proposes a special decoration for women who had well served the nation · George III is formally declared insane !

SIX SHILLINGS (for SEVEN SHILLINGS see page 49)

Obverse DRAPED BUST as English Dollar · Reverse HIBERNIA with HARP
Rev. BANK OF IRELAND TOKEN forming arc above SIX SHILLINGS in exergue.
DATE in exergue, as shown, · Silver 43mm

Date			Fine	V.F.	E.F.	Abt. Unc./FDC
1804	G3/BT61		£40	£200	£500	£750/£950
		(noted 1993)	---	"gd.E.F."	£850	----
		(noted 1997)	"abt.V.F"	£130	----	----
		(noted 1997)		"abt.E.F"	£350	----
1805	G3/BT62	Proof in bronzed copper		----	----	£475/£600
1805	G3/BT63	Proof in gilt copper		----	£600	----/£900
1805	G3/BT64	Proof in silver	----	----	£550	£850/£950

1811 The Prince of Wales and future George IV becomes Prince Regent

1812 More troops called upon to control the Luddite Rising

Typical George III Unofficial Tokens

Listing does not have Fine/VF/EF/Unc etc., but actual 1997 dealers' prices

COPPER except where stated · size virtually exactly as shown

Year	No.	Denomination	Place	Description	Grade	Price
1792	1	Farthing	EDINBURGH	HALF-HALFPENNY	"VF"	£40
1797	2	Farthing	STAFFORD		"EF/gd/EF"	£90
1793	3	Halfpenny	MIDDLESEX	Lace-making	"gdEF"	£45
1794	4	Halfpenny	MIDDLESEX		"E.F."	£25
1794	5	Halfpenny	SLOUGH	Red Lion	"E.F."	£40
1794	6	As previous but in white metal			"E.F."	£90
1795	7	Halfpenny	YORK		"E.F."	£25
1795	8	Halfpenny		Druid's Head/Beehive	"E.F."	£14

No. 1

No. 2

No. 3

No. 4

No. 5

No. 7

No. 8

1813 Wellington, at Vitoria, defeats the French · 21st June

The last gold guinea is minted

Typical George III Unofficial Tokens

Listing does not have Fine/VF/EF/Unc etc., but actual 1997 dealers' prices

COPPER except where stated · size virtually exactly as shown

1795	9	Penny	SUFFOLK	"gdEF"	£125
1797	10	Penny	GLOUCESTER Cathedral	"E.F."	£45
1797	11	Penny	NORWICH "E.F." £50 and	"E.F."	£80
1797	12	Penny	GLOUCESTER	"Unc"	£225
1797	13	Penny	Cardinal Wolsey	"Unc/FDC"	£250
1811	14	Penny	George III	"gd.VF"	£20
1812	15	Penny	DONCASTER	"gd.VF"	£120

No. 9

No. 10

No. 11

No. 12

No. 13

No. 14

No. 15

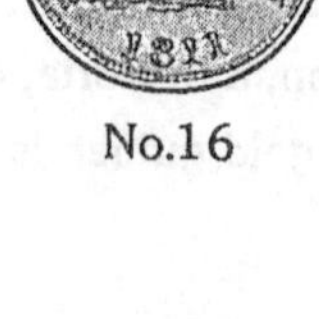

No.16

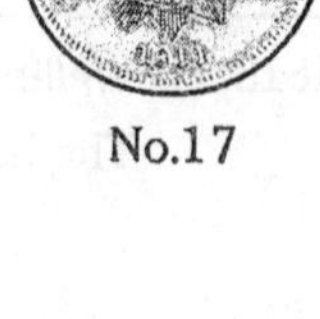

No.17

Listing does not have Fine/VF/EF/Unc etc., but actual 1997 dealers' prices

SILVER except where stated · size virtually exactly as shown

1811	16	Sixpence	YOUNGE & DEAKIN	"gdEF"	£60
1811	17	Sixpence	R. TRIPP & Co.	"E.F."	£45
1811	18	Shilling	N. CORNWALL	"E.F."	£80
1811	19	Shilling	POOLE	"Unc"	£75
1811	20	18d	BERKSHIRE	"gdEF"	£90
1811	21	1/6d	STAMFORD	"gdEF"	£160
1812	22	2/-	NORFOLK	"Unc/FDC"	£500
1811	23	2/6d	READING	"FDC"	£200
1813	24	3/-	JERSEY	"FDC"	£400
1811	25	4/-	BATH (Whitchurch & Dore)	"gdEF"	£240
1811	26	5/-	CHICHESTER	"gdVF"	£1,500

No. 18

No. 19

No.20

No.21

No.22

No.23

No.24

No.25

No.26

BIBLIOGRAPHY

A START TO COIN COLLECTING — Margaret Amstell for W. Foulsham

COINS of ENGLAND and UNITED KINGDOM — The "Seaby's" for B. T. Batsford

COIN NEWS — Monthly Magazine by Token Publications

COLLECTORS COINS: Great Britain — R. J. Marles for Rotographic Publications

COLLECTORS COINS: Ireland — R. J. Marles for Rotographic Publications

ENGLISH COINS — George C. Brooke for Methuen

ENGLISH COPPER, TIN and BRONZE COINS — C. W. Peck for British Museum

ENGLISH MILLED COINAGE — Geoffrey M. Cope and P. Alan Rayner

ENGLISH PROOF and PATTERN CROWN SIZE PIECES
Howard W. A. Linecar and Alex G. Stone for Spink & Son Ltd

ENGLISH SILVER COINAGE — P. Alan Rayner for B. A. Seaby Ltd

GOLD SOVEREIGNS and HALF-SOVEREIGNS — Michael A. Marsh

The MILLED COINAGE of ENGLAND — Spink & Son Ltd

ROYAL SOVEREIGN — G. P. Dyer for Royal Mint

STANDARD CATALOGUE ENGLISH and U.K. COINS
Richard Lobel, Mark Davidson, Allen Hailstone and Elini Calligas

---

BRITISH HISTORY — Rodney Castleden for Paragon

DISCOVERING KINGS and QUEENS — D. E. Wickham for Shire Publications

HISTORY OF THE UNITED STATES Vol.II — Edmund Ollier for Cassell's

KINGS and QUEENS of BRITAIN — David Williamson for Webb & Bower

LIFE and TIMES of GEORGE III — John Clarke for Book Club Associates

---

1814 George Stephenson's first steam locomotive
Abdication of Napoleon · 11th April

George C. Brooke in his "English Coins" (1932 @ 22s 6d) discusses the economic difficulties partly caused by foreign imitations of English coins and the efforts to reform the coinage.

> "In the indentures of this period (1351 to 1399) a clause is always inserted providing for the Trial of the Pyx (box or vase with lid). The Master is instructed to place specimens of every journey weight of coins in a pyx which is to be sealed at the end of three months and sent for trial; a privy mark of the Master's choosing is to be placed on the coins".

He goes on to say that to maintain a 'difference' by which to identify a particular batch whilst retaining costly dies, the 'secret' mark would be struck on the other side of the coin for a second batch and/or, if no confusion was likely, the existing mark would continue as before but with a second mark added to the first.

Even today a Jury is chosen from members of the Goldsmith Company and coins selected at random are put on trial e.g. a sovereign is melted and the ingot assayed in comparison with a Board of trade trial piece. As small a variation as 1/1000th would be frowned on, but typical variations from standard fineness are of the order -0.00009 or minus nine hundred-thousandths ! The Foreman of the Jury will give the Jury's Verdict in the presence of the Queen's Remembrancer.

1814 First cricket match to be held at Lords · 27th June

1815 Napoleon escapes from Elba and builds another army

QUARTER GUINEAS

Date	G3 No.		Fine	V.F.	E.F.	Abt. Uncirc.
			Crowned Garnished Shield · Gold 16mm			
1762	G3/701		£45	£100	£190	£380
1764	G3/702	Patt. Richard Yeo	(Sotheby	1986)	as struck	£1300

1815 Battle of Waterloo, 18th June · Napoleon abdicates again, 22nd June

1816 Lord Elgin sells his 'marbles' to the British Museum

THIRD GUINEAS (seven shillings)

Reverse has large Crown · Silver 17mm

Date	G3 No.		Fine	V.F.	E.F.	Abt. Uncirc.
		FIRST HEAD · GEORGIVS III DEI GRATIA				
		Reverse DATE IN LEGEND: MAG BRI FR ET HIB REX				
1776	G3/705	Patt. Richard Yeo	---	(Spink 1987)	£800	"gd.EF"
1797	G3/706		£45	£75	£150	£300
1798	G3/707		£45	£75	£150	£300
1799	G3/708		£55	£90	£200	£400
1800	G3/709		£45	£75	£150	£300
		Rev. DATE BELOW CROWN: FIDEI DEFENSOR BRITANNIARUM REX				
1801	G3/710		£45	£75	£150	£300
1802	G3/711		£45	£75	£150	£300
1803	G3/712		£45	£75	£150	£300
		SECOND HEAD - SHORT HAIR				
1804	G3/715		£45	£75	£150	£300
1806	G3/716		£45	£75	£150	£300
1808	G3/717		£45	£75	£150	£300
1808		(noted 1997) "A gorgeous little gem"			£125	----
1809	G3/718		£45	£75	£150	£300
1810	G3/719		£45	£75	£150	£300
1811	G3/720		£125	£300	£750	----
1813	G3/721		£70	£150	£300	£650
1813	G3/722	Proof	---	---	----	£1,400

1816 Income Tax is abolished !

1817 First sovereigns are issued · 18th July

HALF GUINEAS

Date	G3 No.		Fine	V.F.	E.F.	Abt. Uncirc.
		FIRST HEAD: curls reach almost to edge · R. Yeo				
		Rev. Crowned Garnished Shield · Crown divides date · Silver 20mm				
1762	801	Pattern by Richard Yeo (Spink 1987) "as struck"				£3,000
1762	802		£225	£600	£1200	----
1763	803		£250	£750	£1500	----
		SECOND HEAD: slightly broader, with shorter hair · R. Yeo				
1764	805		£125	£275	£600	£950
1765	806		£200	£450	£1500	----
1765	807	5 struck over 4	£225	£500	£1600	----
1766	808		£150	£300	£750	£1.200
1768	809		£150	£300	£750	£1.200
1769	810		£125	£275	£600	£950
1772	811	extremely rare	£400	£1200	£3000	----
1773	812		£150	£300	£750	£1.200
1774	813		£225	£500	£1600	----

1817 Java returned to the Dutch

The "Vulcan", the first iron ship, is built on the Clyde

Date	G3 No.		Fine	V.F.	E.F.	Abt. Uncirc.
THIRD HEAD wide space between III and DEI · T. Pingo						
1774	814	extremely rare	£600	£1800	£4000	- - - -
1775	815	see Fourth Head	£250	£500	£1300	- - - -
1775	816	Proof (Spink 1987 "as struck" £2,000) (noted 1997 £5,000)				
FOURTH HEAD more 'regal' looking · (requires careful comparison)						
1775	817	see Third Head	£85	£175	£350	£700
1776	818		£85	£175	£350	£700
1777	819		£85	£175	£350	£700
1778	820		£95	£200	£425	£900
1779	821		£100	£225	£450	£950
Rev. Crowned Garnished Shield · Roman 1 'I' in date · *Silver 20mm*						
1781	822		£95	£200	£425	£900
1783	823		£250	£650	£2000	- - - -
1784	824		£85	£175	£350	£700
1785	825		£85	£175	£350	£700
1786	826		£85	£175	£350	£700

1819 Singapore is 'aquired' by Britain

The future Queen Victoria is born · 24th May

HALF GUINEAS

FIFTH HEAD · L. Pingo · best distinguished by "Spade" reverse

Reverse: Spade-shaped Shield with DATE BELOW SHIELD

Date	G3 No.		Fine	V.F.	E.F.	Abt. Uncirc.
1787	831	Proof, plain edged	----	----	----	£950
1787	832	Proof, in silver !	----	----	----	£700
1787	833		£80	£160	£300	£450
1788	834		£80	£160	£300	£450
1789	835		£80	£160	£300	£450
1790	836		£80	£160	£300	£450
1791	837		£85	£170	£325	£500
1792	838		£350	£750	£1500	----
1793	839		£80	£160	£300	£450
1794	840		£80	£160	£300	£450
1795	841		£80	£160	£300	£450
1796	842		£80	£160	£300	£450
1797	843		£75	£150	£275	£425
1798	844		£75	£150	£275	£425
1798	845	8 struck over 7	£125	£250	£500	----
1800	846		£125	£250	£600	£1,200

SIXTH HEAD · L. Pingo · best distinguished by "Garter" reverse

Reverse: Shield in Crowned Garter · DATE BELOW GARTER

Date	G3 No.		Fine	V.F.	E.F.	Abt. Uncirc.
1801	847		£70	£110	£180	£360
1802	848		£70	£110	£180	£360
1803	849		£70	£110	£180	£360
1803	849	(noted 1997)	----	"VF/gdVF"	£150	----

SEVENTH HEAD · N. Marchant · neater, but date distinguishes

Reverse: Shield in Crowned Garter · DATE BELOW GARTER

Date	G3 No.		Fine	V.F.	E.F.	Abt. Uncirc.
1804	850		£70	£110	£180	£360
1805	851	extremely rare	£450	----	----	----
1806	852		£70	£110	£180	£360
1808	853		£70	£110	£180	£360
1809	854		£70	£110	£180	£360
1810	855		£70	£110	£180	£360
1811	856		£90	£160	£300	£450
1813	857		£85	£150	£280	£425

FIRST HEAD · Richard Yeo · Gold 24mm

Rev. Crowned Ornate Shield · Crown divides date at top · curved 1 in date

Date	G3 No.		Fine	V.F.	E.F.	Abt. Unc.
1761	901		£400	£950	£2000	----
1761	902	Proof (noted 1997)		"E.F."	£3500	----
1761	903	Pattern by J. S. Tanner (Spink 1987)			£3850	----

SECOND HEAD · R. Yeo · curls more abundant at truncation

Date	G3 No.		Fine	V.F.	E.F.	Abt. Unc.
1763	905	Pattern by Yeo (noted 1995)		"gdEF"	£1500	----
1763	906		£300	£700	£1750	----
1764	907		£250	£600	£1500	----
	907	(noted 1997)	----	£320	"V.F. small scrape"	

THIRD HEAD · Richard Yeo · curls reach almost to rim

Date	G3 No.		Fine	V.F.	E.F.	Abt. Unc.
1765	909		£100	£225	£550	----
1766	910		£95	£200	£500	----
1767	911		£100	£225	£550	----
1768	912		£100	£225	£550	----
1769	913		£100	£225	£550	----
1770	914		£125	£250	£600	----
1771	915		£95	£200	£500	----
1772	916		£95	£200	£500	----
1773	917		£95	£200	£500	----

Date	G3 No.	Fine	V.F.	E.F.	Abt. Unc.
		FOURTH HEAD · T. Pingo · larger, laurels reach to edge			
1774	918	£95	£175	£375	----
1775	919	£95	£175	£375	----
1776	920	£95	£176	£375	----
1777	921	£95	£175	£375	----
1778	922	£95	£175	£375	----
1779	923	£95	£175	£375	----
		Rev. Crowned Ornate Shield · Crown divides date · Roman 1 'I' *in date*			
1781	924	£95	£175	£375	----
1782	925	£95	£175	£375	----
1783	926	£120	£240	£480	----
1784	927	£95	£175	£375	----
1785	928	£95	£175	£375	----
1786	929	£85	£160	£325	----

FIFTH HEAD · L. Pingo · Gold 24mm

Reverse has spade-shaped shield · DATE BELOW SHIELD

THE SPADE GUINEA (many forgeries and brass look-alikes)

Date	G3 No.		Fine	V.F.	E.F.	Abt. Unc.
1787	951		£75	£150	£300	£400
	951	(noted 1997)	--- "	"Abt.EF"	£250	----
1787	952	Proof, edge plain, various weights			£1400	£1800
1788	953		£75	£150	£300	£400
1789	954		£75	£150	£300	£400
	954	(noted 1997)	---	"E.F."	£295	----
1790	955		£75	£150	£300	£400
1791	956		£75	£150	£300	£400
	956	(noted 1997)	---	"E.F."	£295	----
1792	957		£75	£150	£300	£400
1793	958		£75	£150	£300	£400
	958	(noted 1997)	---	----	"almost unc."	£350
1794	959		£75	£150	£300	£400
1795	960		£100	£175	£350	£400
	960	(noted 1997)	---	----	"BU scarce"	£380
1796	961		£100	£175	£375	£475
1797	962		£75	£150	£300	£400
1798	963		£75	£150	£300	£400
	963	(noted 1997)	---	"E.F."	£325	----
1798	964	8 struck over 7	£120	£200	£400	£500
1799	965		£120	£200	£400	£500

Date	G3 No.		Fine	V.F.	E.F.	Abt. Unc.

SIXTH HEAD · N. Marchant · Gold 24mm

Reverse has Shield in Crowned Garter · DATE BELOW GARTER

THE MILITARY GUINEA

Date	G3 No.		Fine	V.F.	E.F.	Abt. Unc.
1813	971		£125	£300	£600	£950
	971	(noted 1997)	----	“brilliant uncirculated”		£1,200
1813	972	Proof	----	----	----	£2.000
1813	973	Pattern by L. Pingo: Rev. Flag with National Arms				----
	973	(noted 1986)	----	----	“As struck”	£4,000
1813	974	Pattern by T. Wyon: Rev. Shield and National Emblems				----
	974	(noted 1986)	----	----	“As struck”	£4,000
1813	975	Pattern by T. Wyon: Rev. Shield of Arms			----	----
	975	(noted 1986)	----	----	“As struck”	£3,000

Date	No.				Abt. Uncirc.
		YOUNG HEAD · Gold 31mm			
		Reverse: Crowned Ornate Shield · DATE at top, divided by crown			
1768	G3/1001	Pattern only	Extremely rare		----
	G3/1001	(1974)	Seaby: Douglas-Morris sale	"F.D.C."	£8,000
	G3/1001	(1997)	Seaby: 1997 Catalogue	"F.D.C."	£24,000
1773	G3/1007	Pattern only	Extremely rare		----
	G3/1007	(1974)	Seaby: Douglas-Morris sale	"F.D.C."	£7,000
	G3/1007	(1997)	Seaby: 1997 Catalogue	"F.D.C."	£24,000
1777	G3/1013	Pattern only	Extremely rare		----
	G3/1013	(1974)	Seaby: Douglas-Morris sale	"Nr.F.D.C."	£9,000
	G3/1013	(1997)	Seaby: 1997 Catalogue	"F.D.C."	£24,000

Date	No.				Abt. Uncirc.
		YOUNG HEAD · Gold 37mm			
		Reverse: Crowned Ornate Shield · DATE at top, divided by crown			
1770	G3/1021	Pattern only	Extremely rare		- - - -
	G3/1021	(1974) Seaby: Douglas-Morris sale		"Nr.F.D.C."	£20,000
	G3/1021	(1997) Seaby: 1997 Catalogue		"F.D.C."	£62,000
1773	G3/1027	Pattern only	Extremely rare		- - - -
	G3/1027	(1974) Seaby: Douglas-Morris sale		"F.D.C."	£18,000
	G3/1027	(1997) Seaby: 1997 Catalogue		"F.D.C."	£62,000
1777	G3/1033	Pattern only	Extremely rare		- - - -
	G3/1033	(1974) Seaby: Douglas-Morris sale		"Nr.F.D.C."	£20,000
	G3/1033	(1997) Seaby: 1997 Catalogue		"F.D.C."	£62,000

Date	No.	Mintage etc.	Fine	V.F.	E.F.	Abt. Uncirc.
		LAUREATE HEAD · DATE BELOW HEAD · Gold 19.3mm *Reverse: Crowned Shield · Crown Divides Legend at Top*				
1817	G3/1041	2,080,197	£50	£90	£175	£325
	G3/1041	(noted 1997)	---	---	"EF/Unc"	£280
1817	G3/1042	Proof	---	---	----	£1,750
1818	G3/1043	18 struck over 17	£100	£180	£350	£475
1818	G3/1044	1,030,286	£60	£100	£200	£400
1818	G3/1045	Proof	---	---	----	£4,500
1820	G3/1046	35,043	£65	£110	£225	£375

Date	No.	Mintage etc.	Fine	V.F.	E.F.	Abt. Uncirc.
LAUREATE HEAD · DATE at rim BELOW HEAD · Gold 22.05mm						
Reverse: St.George and The Dragon contained within Inscribed Garter						
1817	G3/1051	3,235,239	£110	£180	£385	£550
1817	G3/1052	Proof	----	----	----	£4,500
1818		2,347,230	Types 'A' and 'B'		----	----
1818	G3/1053	Type 'A'	£120	£220	£500	£750
1818	G3/1054	Type 'B'	£120	£220	£500	£750
1818	G3/1055/6	Proof	----	----	----	£5,500
1818	G3/1057	Type 'A' with "wiry" curls		----	----	----
1818	G3/1058	Type 'B' with "wiry" curls		----	----	----
1819	G3/1059	3,574	but rarer than mintage suggests			----
	G3/1059	(noted 1992)	----	£17,050	"almost V.F."	----
1820	G3/1060	Proof	----	----	----	£1,400
	G3/1060	(noted 1997)	----	----	"F.D.C."	£1,650
1820	G3/1061	931,994	£110	£180	£385	£550
	G3/1061	(noted 1997)	----	"almost EF"	£300	----
1820	G3/1062	"Squat" date	£110	£180	£385	£550
1820	G3/1063	Small '0' in date	£110	£180	£385	£550

Type 'A' has no space between REX and F:D:/colon after BRITANNIA *descends*
Type 'B' has a space between REX and F:D:/colon after BRITANNIA *ascends*

TWO POUNDS (Double Sovereigns)

Date	No.	Mintage etc.	Fine	V.F.	E.F.	Abt. Uncirc.
		LAUREATE HEAD · DATE BELOW HEAD · Gold 27mm *Reverse: St. George and The Dragon · Benedetto Pistrucci*				
1820	G3/1072	Pattern only · 60 pieces		----	----	£12,000

LAUREATE HEAD · DATE BELOW HEAD · Gold 34mm

Reverse: St. George and The Dragon · Benedetto Pistrucci

Date	No.	Mintage etc.	Fine	V.F.	E.F.	Abt. Uncirc.
1820	G3/1075	Pattern E.F. to Abt.FDC			£25,000 to	£35,000
	G3/1075	(noted 1997)	----	----	"FDC"	£55,000

1820 George III dies · Aged 81 · 29th January · The Longest-lived and Longest-reigning King of England · George IV accedes